ICELAND

A TRUE BOOK®

by
Kathleen W. Deady

Children's Press®

A Division of Scholastic Inc.

New York Toronto London Auckland Sydney
Mexico City New Delhi Hong Kong
Danbury, Connecticut

Hikers on the glacier Vatnajökull

Reading Consultant
Sonja I. Smith
Reading Specialist

Content Consultant
Christine Ingebritsen
*Associate Professor of
Scandinavian Studies,
University of Washington*

Library of Congress Cataloging-in-Publication Data

Deady, Kathleen W.
    Iceland / Kathleen W. Deady.
        p. cm. — (A true book)
Summary: Examines the country of Iceland, including its history, people,
arts, festivals, folklore, and recreation.
Includes bibliographical references and index.
    ISBN 0-516-22811-0 (lib. bdg.)   0-516-25832-X (pbk.)
    1. Iceland—Juvenile literature. [1. Iceland.] I. Title. II. Series.
DL305.D43 2004
949.12—dc22

                                                                    2003018660

CHILDREN'S PRESS, and A TRUE BOOK™, and associated logos are
trademarks and or registered trademarks of Scholastic Library Publishing.
SCHOLASTIC and associated logos are trademarks and or registered
trademarks of Scholastic Inc.
3 4 5 6 7 8 9 10 R 13 12 11 10 09 08 07   62

Contents

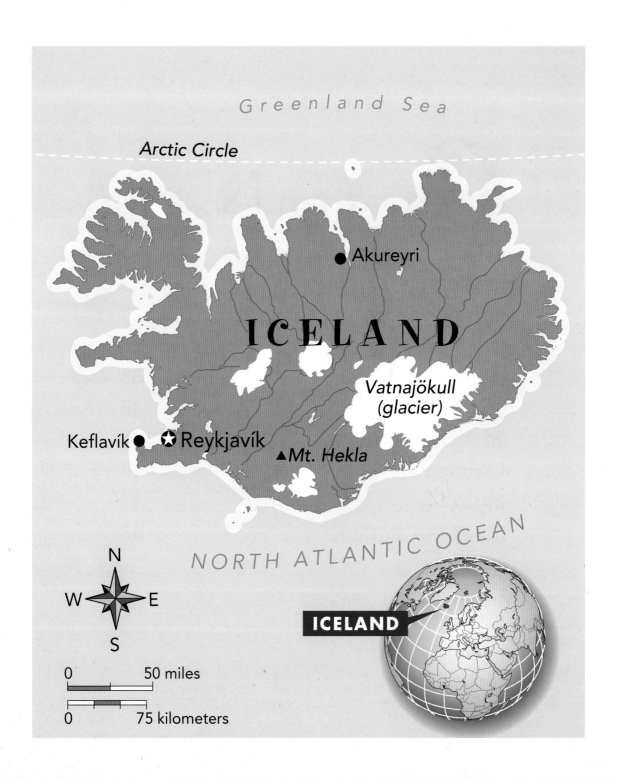

Land of Fire and Ice

Iceland is an island located in the North Atlantic Ocean. Just below the Arctic Circle, Iceland lies about halfway between North America and mainland Europe. Iceland's nearest neighbors are Greenland to the northwest, Norway to the east, and Scotland to the

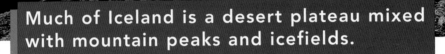

Much of Iceland is a desert plateau mixed with mountain peaks and icefields.

southeast. Iceland covers an area of about 40 square miles (103,000 square kilometers), or a little less than the state of Kentucky.

Much of central Iceland is a barren desert **plateau**. There are very few trees, and the poor soil there cannot be used for grazing animals or growing crops. Large areas are covered with snow and ice fields called **glaciers**. The glacier Vatnajökull in southeast Iceland is the largest in Europe. It is more than 3,000 feet (914 meters) thick in places.

Many volcanoes are scattered throughout the island. When a volcano erupts, it shoots out fiery, melted rock, called lava, from inside the earth. The most famous volcano in Iceland is Mount Hekla in the south.

Red hot lava flows into the sea on the coast of Iceland.

This combination of volcanoes and glaciers gives Iceland its nickname, The Land of Fire and Ice.

Volcanic activity causes many underground hot springs. The water in these springs gets so hot from the lava that sometimes a **geyser** is

formed. Geysers shoot boiling-hot
water or steam high into the air
through cracks in the earth.
Icelanders use the energy from
this underground heat, called
geothermal energy, to heat homes
and pools and to power businesses.

Iceland's central plateau drops to grassy lowlands in coastal areas. Bays and deep narrow inlets, called fjords, cut into much of the coastline. Iceland's sparse wildlife includes the native arctic fox and seabirds called puffins. Mice and reindeer were brought to the island by various groups of settlers.

Iceland's coastline is interrupted by fjords, or narrow inlets of the sea.

Iceland is also known as The Land of the Midnight Sun. In June it is light almost twenty-four hours a day. This is because the North Pole tilts closest toward the sun in that month. In December the North Pole tilts farthest away from the sun, and Iceland is dark for almost the whole month.

Settlement and Survival

Seamen may have known
Iceland existed as early as the
A.D. 300s. However, the first
settlers came from Norway in
A.D. 874. Some also came
from Viking colonies in Britain
and Ireland.

By 930 the population
was about 25,000. Individual

Viking ships braved uncharted seas and explored new lands, including Iceland.

settlements had formed groups, called things, to settle disputes among families. A local **chieftain** ruled each thing.

In 930 the chieftains came together at Thingvellir to form one large governing group, or assembly. This assembly, called the Althing, established a **constitution** and a representative form of government. The Althing was the world's first such governing body.

The early Icelandic settlers worshipped many gods and goddesses. Slowly, Christian settlers came to Iceland. They introduced the Roman

Christian missionaries, or priests, sailed to faraway places to spread their religion.

Catholic religion, which worshipped one god. By around 1000 the Althing adopted Christianity as the state religion.

Erik the Red

Viking Erik Thorvaldson, called Erik the Red, was one of Iceland's early settlers. He arrived there with his family in A.D. 960, after his father was exiled from Norway for killing a man. In 982 Erik himself killed two men, and he was exiled from Iceland for three years. Erik traveled west to an island that he named Greenland, and later began Greenland's first settlement. In 1000 his son Leif Eriksson sailed west to North America. He sailed down the coast and landed in an area he named Vinland. Today, it is known as Newfoundland.

Erik the Red fought and killed an Icelandic chief. He was forced to leave Iceland as a result.

Iceland remained an independent **republic** for more than two hundred years. Icelanders raised livestock and fished. They traded with Europe for grain and other goods. By the 1200s fighting began among the local chieftains. In 1262 the Althing voted to allow Norway to rule Iceland. Then in 1380 Iceland and Norway were taken over by Denmark, a country in northern Europe.

Icelanders struggled to survive when the Black Death struck.

The years that followed were difficult for many people in Iceland. The Black Death struck from 1402 to 1404. This widespread disease killed about one-third of the people in Iceland. Then in the 1600s and 1700s, Denmark created strict trade laws for Iceland, forcing Icelanders to pay high prices for food goods. These unfair trade rules made life difficult for Icelanders, and many people fell into poverty.

From 1783 to 1786 Iceland had the worst volcanic eruptions in its history. The eruption of Laki volcano in south central Iceland caused the most damage. It lasted for eight months between 1783 and 1784.

The Skogar Folk Museum contains information about Iceland's history.

Lava covered the land, destroying livestock, crops, and farmland. As a result, Icelanders did not have enough food, and many starved to death.

Independence to Prosperity

Life in Iceland slowly improved in the 1800s. Iceland remained under Danish rule. However, Icelanders grew increasingly unhappy with this situation. They wanted more independence.

Although the Danish king had stopped the Althing meetings in 1800, they were resumed

in 1843. Icelanders continued to demand the right to govern themselves. Over time, Iceland gained representation in the Danish government.

In 1874 Denmark gave Iceland its own constitution in honor of its one-thousandth anniversary. The constitution gave Iceland more say in its own affairs, including control over its own money. In 1918

King Christian X of Denmark (right) served as the leader of Iceland from 1912 to 1943.

Iceland became a self-governing kingdom, with its own flag, though it remained united with Denmark under a common king.

The 1900s brought steady growth and progress toward full independence. Other countries had ruled Iceland for seven centuries. Finally, on June 17, 1944, the citizens voted for independence. The Republic of Iceland is now governed by a prime minister and a president.

After becoming independent in 1944, Iceland's first president was Sveinn Bjornsson, shown here giving a speech.

Women have played increasingly important roles in the growth of Iceland. In 1980 Icelanders elected Vigdis Finnbogadottir president, the first woman ever elected president of a republic. Ólafur Ragnar Grímsson replaced her as president in 1996. Today, Iceland has one of the highest standards of living in the world.

Icelanders Today

Icelanders descend from the original northern European settlers. They are generally tall, blond, and light-skinned. Immigration from other countries is limited, so there are very few ethnic minorities.

Iceland is the most thinly populated country in Europe,

with fewer than 300,000 people. More than half the people live in and around Reykjavík, the capital and largest city. The rest of the population lives in smaller cities and towns, or in rural areas.

Most homes in Iceland are built of strengthened concrete. This helps homes stand up to earthquakes and high coastal winds. Icelanders often paint their homes pastel, or light, colors.

The city of Reykjavík (above) is filled with colorful row houses (right).

Icelanders enjoy a healthy, comfortable lifestyle. Homes are well equipped with modern appliances and electronics.

A family in Iceland enjoys a home-cooked meal.

At meals, Icelanders often eat fish or lamb, fresh as well as smoked, dried, or pickled. Special foods include pickled shark and boiled sheep's head.

Most Icelanders are well educated, and almost everyone can read. Their language, called

Icelandic, comes from Old Norse and is similar to Norwegian. The Icelandic alphabet has some letters from the English alphabet, and several others to represent other sounds. Many Icelanders also speak both English and Danish, the language of Denmark.

Many students use computers both at home and at school.

Icelandic Names

The practice of using *son* or *dottir* for children's names is a family tradition in Iceland.

Icelanders do not have family last names. Children are given a first name and their second name is taken from their father's name. To that second name they add *son* if it is a boy and *dottir* if it is a girl. For example, a man named Jonas has a son Karl. Karl would be Karl Jonasson, meaning son of Jonas. His daughter Inga would be Inga Jonasdottir, daughter of Jonas. What would your name be in Iceland?

Work and Recreation

Iceland's cost of living is high. Many goods are expensive because they must be bought from other countries. People often work long hours and hold two jobs.

Iceland's economy depends largely on the sea, its most important natural resource.

About twelve in every one hundred Icelanders fish or work in fish processing.

Coastal waters hold many fish, including cod, haddock, capelin, and herring. Fish, and whale products such as meat and oil, make up almost three-quarters of Iceland's **exports** to other countries. Many people work in factories, making clothing, food products, and chemical and electrical products. Government and tourism jobs have also become very important.

A small number of Icelanders are farmers. Farmers raise sheep for meat and wool, cattle for dairy products, and chickens for eggs. They grow potatoes and

Farmers baling hay

turnips, and hay for their animals. Some grow cabbage, lettuce, carrots, and tomatoes in greenhouses heated with geothermal energy.

Icelanders like to stay active. Most Icelanders are strong and physically fit. As a result, they are good in sports, such as weight lifting, that require great strength. Glima, similar to Japanese sumo wrestling, is a traditional form of Icelandic wrestling.

Icelanders also like to read and play games. Bridge is a favorite card game, and chess is very popular. The famous 1972 world chess championship took place in Reykjavík.

The Arts, Folktales, and Festivals

Iceland is well known for its **literature**. In the 1100s and 1200s, the Golden Age of Literature, authors wrote sagas of heroes, kings, and gods. Sagas were long tales of Icelandic heroes. A famous Icelandic author,

Snorri Sturluson (c.1179–1241), wrote *Heimskringla*, the greatest of the sagas. The Icelandic language has changed little over the centuries. Most Icelanders can still read the original sagas.

In recent years the arts have developed in other ways as well. Icelandic films and popular singers such as Björk and Sigur Rós have become known around the world. Actors, dancers, and musicians perform throughout Iceland. The number of artists is growing.

Icelandic folktales are filled with stories of mermaids, sea monsters, elves, trolls, and ghosts. At Christmastime, children believe Yuletide Lads visit homes every night for thirteen nights. They are

The Icelandic Symphony Orchestra

The lighting of the town Christmas tree

said to be the elf children of a mean troll woman named Gryla. The lads cause mischief, slamming doors and stealing candles. They leave a gift for good children in a shoe placed by the window.

Icelanders celebrate many other holidays and festivals. Fireworks and bonfires light up the long hours of darkness on New Year's Eve. On June 17, parades mark Iceland's National Day, the day when its citizens

A marching-band drummer takes part in a National Day parade in Reykjavík.

voted for independence in 1944. Street theater and music take place all day long. Icelanders enjoy many occasions to celebrate their long history and rich traditions.

To Find Out More

Here are some additional resources to help you learn more about Iceland:

 **Books**

Brimner, Larry Dane. **Glaciers.** Children's Press, 2000.

Gentle, Victor, and Janet Perry. **Volcanoes.** Gareth Stevens Publishing, 2004.

Graham, Ian S. **Geothermal and Bio-Energy.** Raintree/Steck Vaughn, 1999.

Rodgers, Mary M., editor. **Iceland in Pictures.** Lerner Publications, 1996.

Organizations and Online Sites

Iceland Naturally
http://www.icelandnaturally.com/abouticeland.shtml

This site gives lots of basic information on the history, government, education, population, and industry of Iceland.

Embassy of Iceland in Washington, D.C.
http://www.iceland.org/us/

This site offers information about the economy, government, and history of Iceland.

Iceland Tourist Board
http://www.icelandtouristboard.com/

This site includes just about everything you might want to know about Iceland, including facts, photos, and fun things to do there.

Important Words

chieftain the chief or head of a tribe or clan

constitution a formal set of laws and principles to govern by

exports goods and services one country produces and sells to others

geothermal coming from the heat inside Earth

geyser a spring that sometimes shoots up hot water and steam

glaciers large bodies of ice that cover an area or that slowly move

literature written works

plateau a raised, flat area of land

republic a form of government in which the power is with the people and the representatives they elect

Index

Meet the Author

Kathleen W. Deady has written more than thirty books for children. They include picture books and non-fiction books on a variety of topics. Her work has also appeared in several children's magazines. She has worked as a preschool teacher and director, as well as a special education tutor in elementary schools.

Kathleen lives in Manchester, New Hampshire, with her husband, Bill; daughter, Erin; and son, Matthew. When she isn't writing, she enjoys singing in a local women's singing group, as well as gardening, camping, biking, and feeding birds.